D1476607

Hiroshi Watanabe

Findings

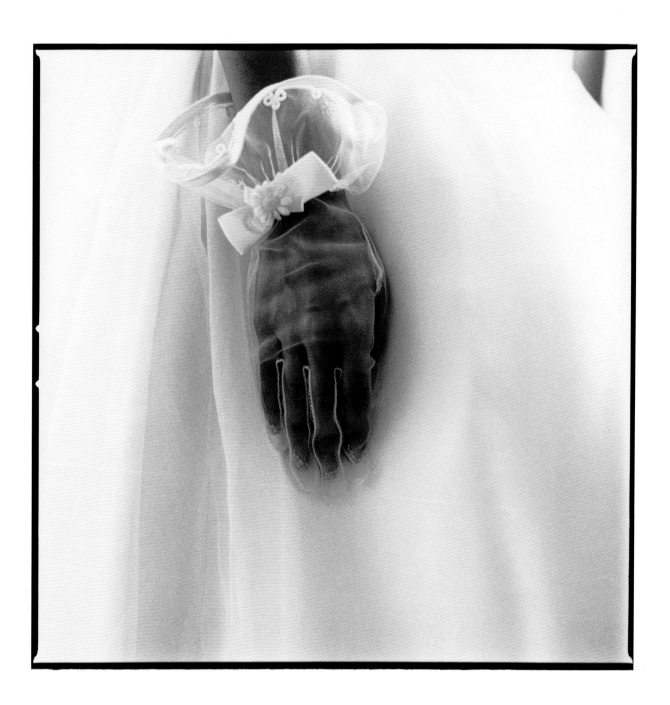

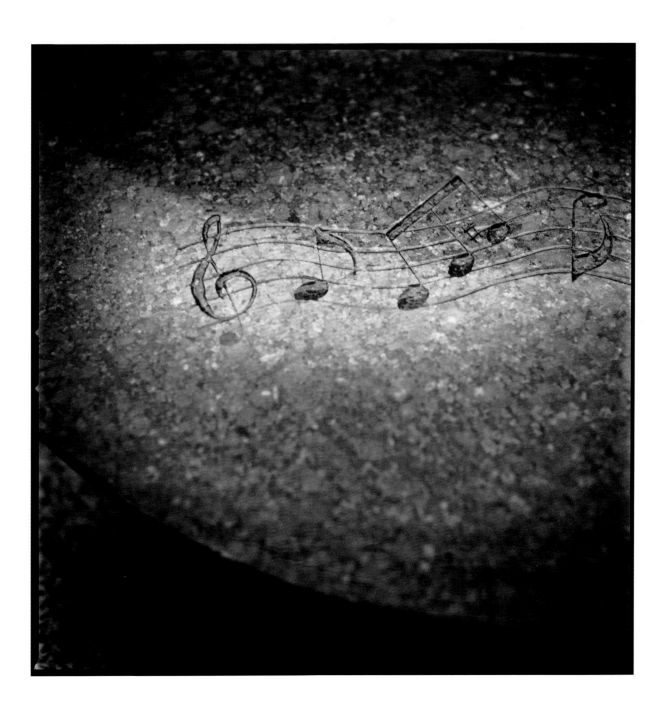

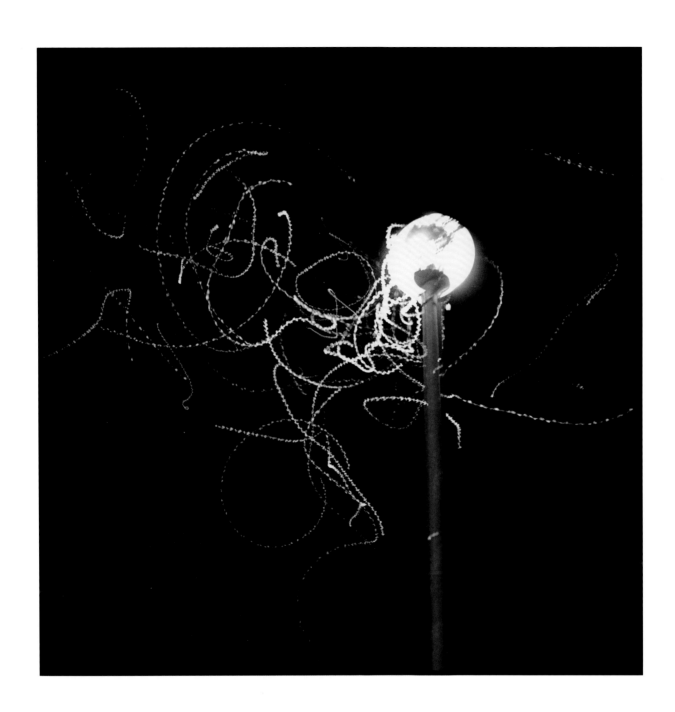

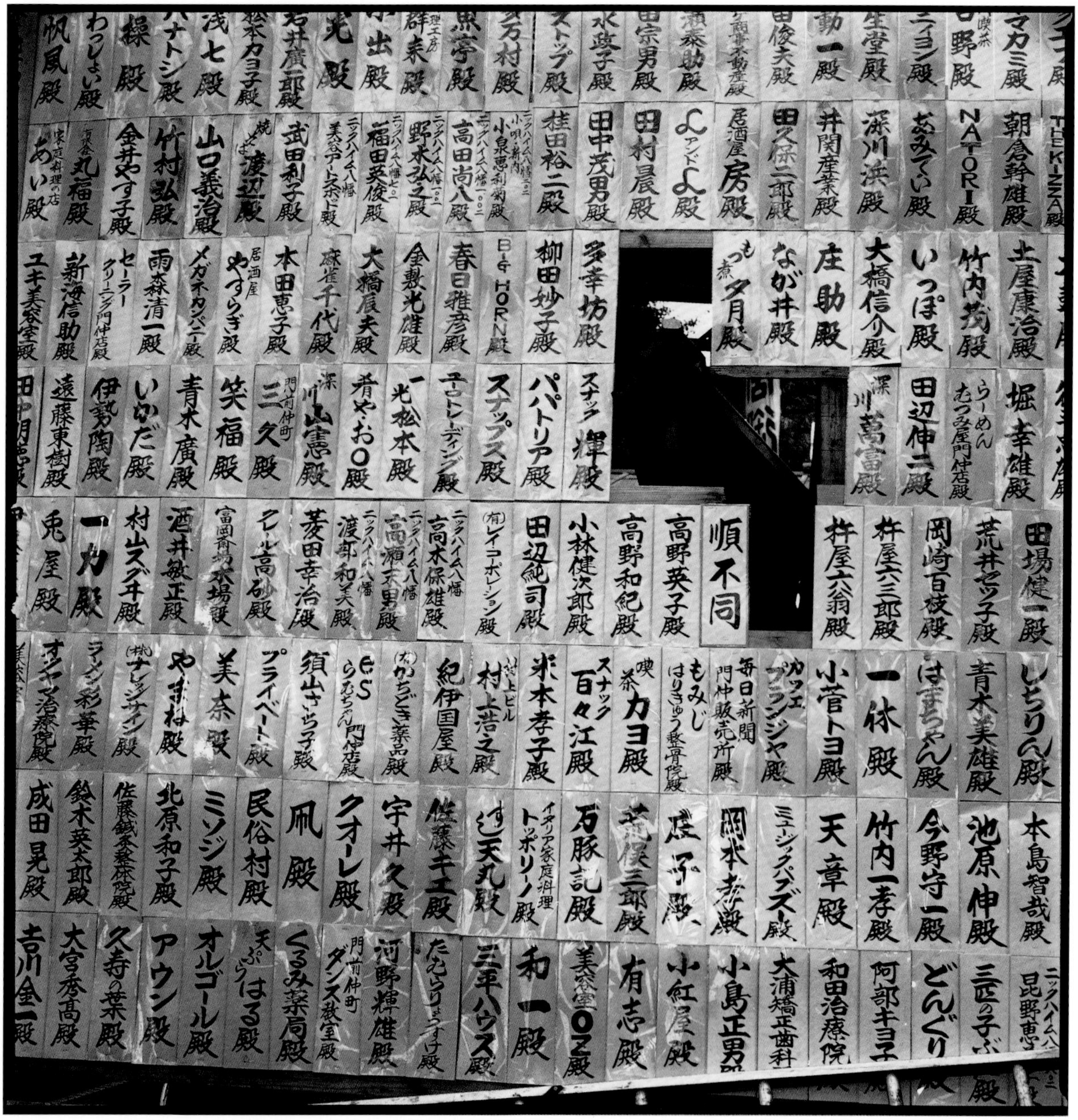

Page 1 – El Arbolito Park, Quito, Ecuador, 2002
Page 5 – Agra Fort, India, 2000
Page 6 – Ellis Island, New York, 1999
Page 7 – Bakery Window, Lerma, Spain, 2005
Page 8 – Barber Shop, Asakusa, Japan, 2004
Page 9 – Baseball Field, Tokyo University, Japan, 2004
Page 10 – Quito, Ecuador 3, 2000
Page 11 – Quito, Ecuador 4, 2000
Page 12 – Wedding Glove, Honolulu, Hawaii, 2004
Page 13 – White Terns, Midway Atoll, 1999
Page 14 – Music Notes, Nakatsugwa, Japan, 2003
Page 15 – Museu d'Art Contemorani de Barcelona, Spain, 2005
Page 16 – Battery Park, New York, 1999
Page 17 – Blue Lagoon 2, Iceland, 1999
Page 18 – Sata Monica Pier, 2000
Page 19 – Coliseo Gallo de Oro 1, 2001
Page 20 – Church Flower, San Lazaro Psychiatric Hospital, 2001
Page 21 – Blue Lagoon, Iceland, 1999
Page 22 – Mt. Popa, Burma, 1998
Page 23 – Mandalay, Burma, 1998
Page 24 – Quito, Ecuador 9, 2000
Page 25 – Santa Rosa Farm, Ecuador, 2000
Page 26 – Sardar Market, Jodhpur, India, 2000
Page 27 – Spider Web, Kameido, Japan, 2005
Page 28 – Street Lamp, Los Angeles, 1997
Page 28 – Summer Bugs, Furano Prince Hotel, Japan, 2004
Page 30 – Vietnam War Memorial, Washington DC, 1999
Page 31 – Butterflies, Ishigaki Island, Japan, 2000
Page 32 – Hokkaido Historical Village, Japan, 2004
Page 33 – Kaneiji Gojunotou, Tokyo, Japan, 2006
Page 34 – Shinobazu Bentendo, Tokyo, Japan, 2004
Page 35 – Christmas Tree, Fairbanks, Alaska, 1997
Page 36 – Calico, California, 2001
Page 37 – Atore Ueno, Tokyo, Japan, 2006
Page 38 – Raw Silk, Meiji Village, Japan, 2005
Page 39 – Kemeido Jingu, Tokyo, Japan, 2005
Page 40 – Pachinko Parlor, Tokyo, Japan, 2005
Page 41 – Waikiki Beach, Hawaii, 2001
Page 42 – American Museum of Natural History, New York, 2002
Page 43 – Hoover Dam, Nevada, 2001
Page 44 – Noboribetsu, Japan, 2003
Page 45 – Wall Street, New York, 1999
Page 46 – Bubble Man, New York, 1996
Page 47 – Commercial Ibarra, Ecuador, 2002
Page 48 – Quito, Ecuador 2, 2002
Page 49 – Bourbon Street, New Orleans, 2001
Page 50 – Tsutenkaku, Osaka, Japan, 2003
Page 51 – Toris Bar, Yokohama, Japan, 2002
Page 52 – Crow, Kiyosumi Garden, Japan, 2004
Page 53 – Hakodate Fish Market, Japan, 2003
Page 54 – Tomioka Hachimangu, Tokyo, Japan, 2005
Page 55 – Aichi, Japan, 2005
Page 56 – Yasukuni Jinja 1, Japan, 2005
Page 57 – Yasukuni Jinja 2, Japan, 2005
Page 58 – Tobu Land, Japan, 2005
Page 59 – Himeji Castle, Japan, 2006
Page 61 – Bora Bora, Tahiti, 1997

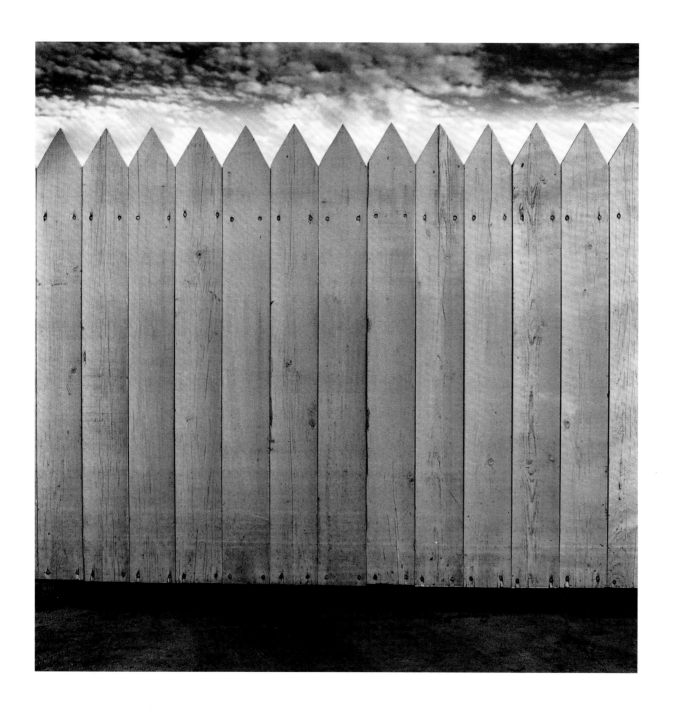

Silence

Some photographs communicate with a look, a sharp glance, as a disapproval at the dinner table, or upon an interruption of a thought. Some photographs are fragrant, like a breeze, or a bonfire. And some photographs are silent, without words or breath, still, as if outside of time. Then there are noisy children in the park, the sound of a saxophone on Bourbon Street, or rain on the window.

Hiroshi Watanabe's photographs ask a lot of their viewer; they summon full engagement, sometimes implicating other senses, sometimes patiently silent, always refusing to let well enough alone. It is about having the confidence of a practice, a way of being in the world, of shaping one's purpose toward discovery, of waiting until it happens, really happens.

These are modest means, though, and when it is all snapped and done, his work is rarely over-reaching. A fish wrapped transparently, and that is all.

One child climbing through a maze of joined, fashioned poles, climbing toward the sky, not many children, just one, and nothing more than the maze and the clearing in the clouds beyond. This is the photography of an artist who has worked through his language of vision, finding the shape of his grammar, now selecting his words carefully, as if each picture were often a word, just a single word.

Earlier, for twenty-five years, Watanabe made commercials, and in this business, he needed to listen to the language of others without expressing his own personal thoughts. But it was Watanabe's inner self which spoke in a louder voice and changed him. Watanabe then went on to working for himself allowing his inner thoughts and images to prevail.

His images are like words, for they are singular ideas, discovered, rendered, held, understood and shared now with personal, artistic integrity. The pictures are a single frame in the film, not confounded by the contexts of drawn out time, the passages that film unreels from within its time base. The images reflect a single moment, and it is hoped that they are understood that way: The bridge arching into the fog, a reflecting wall that holds the names of the fallen where dead leaves accumulate.

These are honest and direct pictures; they bear a heavy silence, and are uncomplicated, singular ideas. These words invite a closer look uncompromised by time. They suggest a meditation that can bring to the surface what could otherwise have remained hidden - that opening in the sky beyond the child and his maze, and what it can mean.

Watanabe keeps it simple and uncomplicated so that his wisdom can emerge without anything getting in the way. The artist uses the same film, paper, chemicals, camera and lens, as well as the same square format, every time. He insists that nothing be out of the ordinary; no embellishments of technique in printing or in developing; no auxiliaries in the exposures. By these means, the image itself can be and is extraordinary.

Watanabe's work is like a contemplative behavior that focuses on the breath so that the moment is fully free to emerge. So that the instant is lived as completely as it can be, Watanabe stays open for all the elements of discovery - the dried leaves in the foreground before the names of the dead. These are the illuminations of his pictures. And their secret - both in their making and their receiving - is to know what one is doing, to slow down the flickering eye, to draw down deeply into the image, where resides the concept behind the word, and the wisdom behind the concept, and the silence that comes from fine art.

Anthony Bannon
Director, George Eastman House
Rochester, New York

Sometimes what is not seen defines what's most important, gives form to the places and moments where words fail us. And within those places rest our stories, as told through the simplicity of daily life.

Hiroshi Watanabe walks down streets in various corners of the world and finds these stories. His gift is in noticing the quiet in between and through his images, showing us how that feels. His softly-edged observations reflect a world laced with metaphor, quiet scenes, human interactions, that weave together forming the fabric of lives lived.

As the first Book Prize of Photolucida's Critical Mass competition, Watanabe is honored by the judges for his unique way of seeing. More than 560 photographers from around the world entered, and 250 judges made their selections. Two additional book prizes were awarded to Louie Palu and Sage Sohier.

Critical Mass, and indeed all the projects of Photolucida, are at their root about connecting people. The portfolio review event gives an opportunity for direct dialogue between photographers and industry professionals. Critical Mass allows artist projects to pass in front of the eyes of a large and varied international group of curators, publishers, and gallery owners.

Within this book is a different kind of interaction, one occurring with each turn of the page. It is fitting that the first-ever Critical Mass book is awarded to an artist such as Watanabe, whose elegant images are filled with such lingering resonance that they practically slip off the page. We hope you enjoy discovering all he has found.

Kirsten Rian
Board Chair, Photolucida
Executive Director, The Aftermath Project

As part of photolucida's Critical Mass,
Hiroshi Watanabe, Sage Sohier and
Louis Palu were each awarded
monographs by a group of 200 jurors
comprised of some of the most
important photography curators in
the world.
To find out more about photolucida,
Critical Mass, the other two
monographs and our Portland
portfolio reviews go to:
www.photolucida.org
©2007 photolucida, Portland, Oregon,
Images copyrighted by Hiroshi
Watanabe, Text copyrighted by
Anthony Bannon and Kirsten Rian.
All rights reserved.
ISBN 978-1-934334-00-3